HOW IS IT [
ICE CReAM

by R.J. Bailey

pogo

Ideas for Parents and Teachers

Pogo Books let children practice reading informational text while introducing them to nonfiction features such as headings, labels, sidebars, maps, and diagrams, as well as a table of contents, glossary, and index.

Carefully leveled text with a strong photo match offers early fluent readers the support they need to succeed.

Before Reading

- "Walk" through the book and point out the various nonfiction features. Ask the student what purpose each feature serves.
- Look at the glossary together. Read and discuss the words.

Read the Book

- Have the child read the book independently.
- Invite him or her to list questions that arise from reading.

After Reading

- Discuss the child's questions. Talk about how he or she might find answers to those questions.
- Prompt the child to think more. Ask: What is your favorite kind of ice cream? What is your favorite way to eat it?

Pogo Books are published by Jump!
5357 Penn Avenue South
Minneapolis, MN 55419
www.jumplibrary.com

Library of Congress Cataloging-in-Publication Data

Names: Bailey, R.J., author.
Title: Ice cream: how is it made? / by R.J. Bailey.
Description: Minneapolis, Minnesota: Jump!, Inc. 2016.
Series: How is it made? | Includes index.
Identifiers: LCCN 2016037288 (print)
LCCN 2016038184 (ebook)
ISBN 9781620315682 (hardcover: alk. paper)
ISBN 9781620316085 (pbk.)
ISBN 9781624965166 (ebook)
Subjects: LCSH: Ice cream, ices, etc.–Juvenile literature.
Classification: LCC TX795 .B33 2016 (print)
LCC TX795 (ebook) | DDC 641.86/2–dc23
LC record available at https://lccn.loc.gov/2016037288

Editor: Jenny Fretland VanVoorst
Designer: Leah Sanders
Photo Researcher: Leah Sanders

Photo Credits: All photos by Shutterstock except:
Adobe Stock, 16-17; Alamy, 12-13, 18; Getty, 5, 6, 8-9, 19; iStock, cover, 10-11, 20-21.

Printed in the United States of America at Corporate Graphics in North Mankato, Minnesota.

TABLE OF CONTENTS

CHAPTER 1

A COLD, CREAMY TREAT

What is your favorite summer treat? Is it cold? Is it creamy? It must be ice cream!

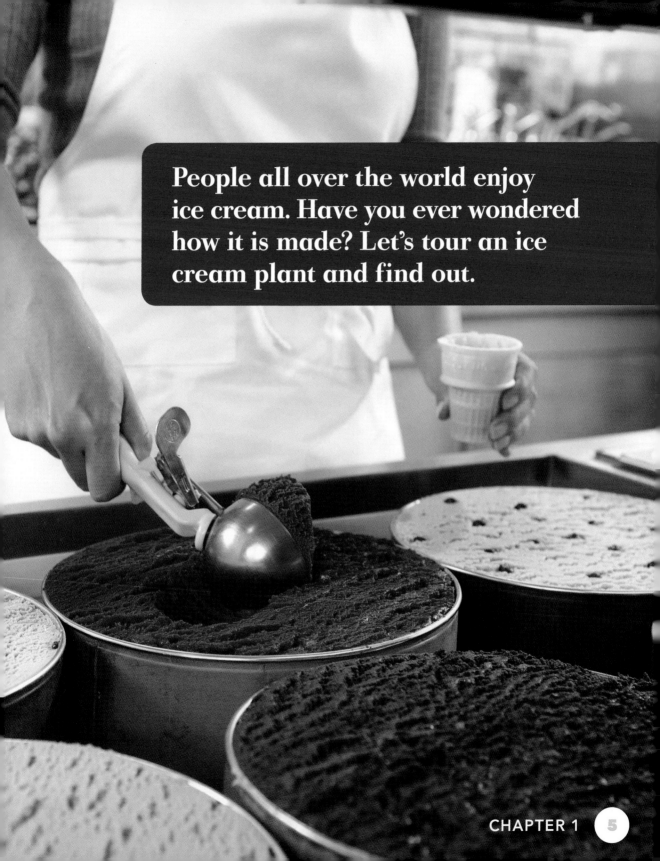

People all over the world enjoy ice cream. Have you ever wondered how it is made? Let's tour an ice cream plant and find out.

CHAPTER 2

AT THE PLANT

Ice cream begins with milk. Workers load milk from dairy farms onto refrigerated trucks. The trucks bring it to the ice cream plant.

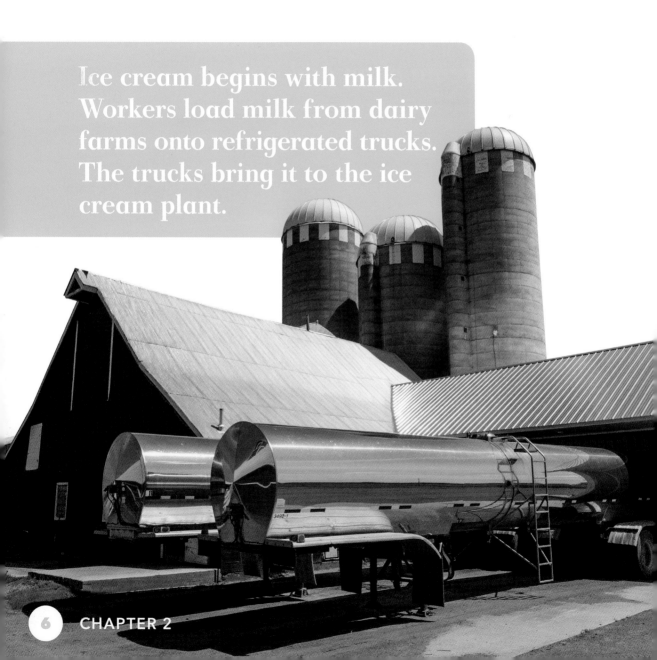

At the plant, the milk is pumped into large tanks. The tanks are kept at 36 degrees Fahrenheit (2 degrees Celsius).

The milk goes into blenders. Workers add sugar and other **ingredients** such as eggs, salt, and **stabilizers**.

DID YOU KNOW?

Ice cream must contain at least 10 percent fat. If there is less than that, the ice cream will not be smooth. It will taste icy.

Once blended, the mix goes into a **pasteurizer**. This machine runs the cold mix through a series of heated pipes. The process kills **bacteria** that may be in the mix.

DID YOU KNOW?

In 1864, French scientist Louis Pasteur found that heat could kill bacteria. The process he invented is called pasteurization. It makes milk and other foods safe to eat.

Look! The mix goes into a **homogenizer**. The mix enters a tube. It is forced out with high pressure. The pressure makes the ice cream smoother.

TAKE A LOOK!

A homogenizer uses pressure to make ice cream smoother.

① Ice cream mix is fed into the machine.
② The milk fat is squashed.
③ The smoother mixture is pushed out.

The mix goes to a tank room. It rests for four to eight hours. This cools the mix. At this stage, workers add flavors and colors.

DID YOU KNOW?

Some people get "brain freeze" when they eat ice cream. The cold makes blood vessels in the head cool and shrink. The headache comes when they warm up again. The blood vessels swell, sending pain signals to the brain.

After resting, the mix goes to the freezer. Air is pumped into the mix. This increases the ice cream's **volume**. When the mix leaves the freezer, it is still soft. A machine called a feeder adds items such as fruit, candy, and nuts. A blender mixes these large pieces into the soft ice cream.

DID YOU KNOW?

Cones became popular in 1904. An ice cream seller at the St. Louis World's Fair ran out of dishes. A waffle maker wanted to help. He rolled his waffles into cones.

CHAPTER 3

FINAL STEPS

EXP 26 03 17

expiration date

A filling machine fills cartons with ice cream. It puts lids on them. It pushes the cartons onto a **conveyor belt**. An **expiration date** is printed onto each one.

The belt moves the ice cream to a hardening room. The room is set to about -20 degrees F (-29 degrees C). The ice cream freezes.

The frozen ice cream goes to cold warehouses. Workers load trucks. They bring the ice cream to stores. It is ready to eat! Who wants an ice cream cone?

TAKE A LOOK!

How does milk become ice cream?

Blending

Smoothing

Freezing

Heating

Resting

Filling

ACTIVITIES & TOOLS

ICE CREAM IN A BAG

**It is easy to make ice cream at home.
You will need:**

- ½ cup whole milk or half and half
- ½ tsp vanilla
- 1 Tbsp sugar
- 4 cups crushed ice
- 4 Tbsp salt
- 2 quart-sized sealable plastic bags
- 1 gallon-sized sealable freezer bag

❶ Mix the milk, vanilla, and sugar in one of the quart bags. Squeeze out any extra air and close it tightly.

❷ Place this bag inside the other quart bag. Again, squeeze out any extra air and close it tightly.

❸ Put this double bag inside the gallon bag. Fill the remaining space in the gallon bag with ice. Sprinkle salt on the ice. Remove any extra air and close the bag tightly.

❹ Shake the gallon bag for five to 10 minutes. Make sure the ice surrounds the cream mix.

❺ Your ice cream is ready! It will be soft. Add nuts or candy or cookie pieces if you'd like. Enjoy!

GLOSSARY

bacteria: Tiny life forms that can be dangerous if eaten.

conveyor belt: A moving band of rubber or metal used for moving objects from one place to another.

expiration date: The date after which manufacturers recommend a food not be eaten.

homogenizer: A machine that makes the balls of milk fat in ice cream smaller, thereby making the ice cream smooth.

ingredients: The things that are added in a mix to make ice cream and other foods.

pasteurizer: A machine that heats milk and other liquids to kill bacteria.

stabilizers: Substances that slow the growth of ice crystals in ice cream.

volume: An amount of something.

INDEX

TO LEARN MORE

Learning more is as easy as 1, 2, 3.

1) Go to www.factsurfer.com

2) Enter "icecream" into the search box.

3) Click the "Surf" button to see a list of websites.

With factsurfer, finding more information is just a click away.